MANAGING DIVERSITY:

WORDS INTO ACTIONS

Dr Gary Mulh

Dr Mustafa Ö

Dianah Worr

First published 2006

Cover and text design by Sutchinda Rangsi-Thompson
Typeset by Paperweight
Printed in Great Britain by Antony Rowe

British Library Cataloguing in Publication Data
A catalogue record for this book is available from the British Library

ISBN   1 84398 168 8
ISBN-13   978 1 84398 168 8

Chartered Institute of Personnel and Development,
151 The Broadway, London SW19 1JQ

Tel: 020 8612 6200
Website: www.cipd.co.uk

Incorporated by Royal Charter. Registered charity no. 1079797.

CONTENTS

ACKNOWLEDGEMENTS

The CIPD is grateful to all those who took part in the diversity action research programme.

FOREWORD

It is argued that people are the single most important source of competitive advantage. Research by the Chartered Institute of Personnel and Development, *Understanding the people and performance link: Unlocking the black box*, provides empirical evidence to show the relationship of good people management and business performance, while the CIPD guide, *Managing diversity: people make the difference at work – but everyone is different*, sets out the evidence about the importance of valuing *individual differences* in managing people.

The message about the importance of managing diversity as a mainstream business issue is getting louder, as the global marketplace grows and competition becomes more intense. The ability to increase the added value that each employee contributes to business performance is vital to improving productivity, as are ways of meeting the needs and preferences of a diverse marketplace to improve market share.

Alongside these pressures, UK discrimination law is becoming more extensive and people's expectations about values, ethics and fair treatment at work are becoming more sophisticated. International trends also suggest that discrimination law is likely to intensify and broaden in the future.

All of these issues raise questions about the viability of traditional working practices, rigid workplace cultures and how people relate to each other at work. They create an appetite for more knowledge about managing diversity, how it can support the delivery of business goals and how to make progress beyond the compliance-based guidance that helps to keep employers out of the law courts.

The Chartered Institute of Personnel and Development (CIPD) has produced a range of research and guidance documents in order to raise awareness and improve understanding about managing diversity. This new report describes a unique, longitudinal action-based research study, designed to explore how people responsible for progressing diversity in their organisations make things happen.

It explores some of the practical challenges faced by employers in dealing with diversity issues and describes the solutions that they have formulated. It includes recommendations that are rooted in the experiences of nine different organisations from the public, private and voluntary sectors. The report also outlines how participation in the research helped those organisations to design and implement diversity management initiatives that progressed change by challenging the status quo.

Traditionally, organisations' concerns over the accommodation of individual and group-based differences have been resolved through equality initiatives, striving to deliver 'fairness'. However, in today's environment, evidence is emerging that consumers and employees alike do not want to fit into management-, or business-driven pigeon-holes. They want to be accepted as unique individuals – distinctive – not segmented or labelled according to their identification with social groups. This is also in line with the decline of solidarity and the rise of individualism in both organisations and society.

Managing diversity is based on recognising and valuing people as individuals and acknowledging that differences need to be addressed and managed as part of a continuous process of organisational change, in ways that are integral to the delivery of business goals.

However, there are no quick fixes or one-size-fits-all solutions to managing diversity, because the challenges presented reflect organisational and personal contexts, circumstances, needs and preferences – all of which change over time. Therefore, diversity management is not about identifying an unchanging set of individual differences, but about recognising and benefiting from individual difference as an outcome of dynamic changes in individual experiences, needs, aspirations and interactions in the context of work and organisation.

In the same way, experience shows that managing diversity is an ongoing challenge involving continuous learning, constant change and moving goalposts. While some organisations are struggling to start their journey, others are committed and involved. Sharing and stimulating learning about making progress is imperative in order to stop the unnecessary reinvention of the wheel and to build knowledge and good practice.

This report contains some valuable insights about getting out of the starting blocks in order to progress diversity and maintain momentum. It describes how the CIPD designed a group action research programme to help participating organisations make progress in ways that were focused and relevant to their business challenges, by using fact-finding research, discussion and reflection to design and implement customised solutions.

Dianah Worman, OBE, Chartered FCIPD
CIPD Adviser, Diversity

EXECUTIVE SUMMARY

This report of a longitudinal action research study into managing diversity shares the concerns, joy, pain and experience of a group of managers from different backgrounds and disciplines, who were brought together in a learning adventure. Representatives from nine different organisations from the public, private and voluntary sectors, worked together as a collective unit of discovery in the action research programme. The following organisations, some of which are anonymous, took part in the programme:

From the public sector

Stockport Metropolitan Borough Council
Government Department X
Government Department Y
Government Department Z

From the private sector

HBOS plc
Ford Europe
Barclays Bank plc
Tesco plc

From the voluntary sector

WRVS

The programme involved setting up an Action Research Group (ARG) made up of people with different backgrounds, perspectives and approaches, to solve and practise aspects of diversity management relevant to them and the different organisations they represented.

The ARG was facilitated and recorded by academic advisers and organisational change specialists and co-ordinated by the CIPD.

Participation was self-funded, and the greatest asset contributed was the time and enthusiasm of the nine diversity managers from the delegate organisations.

The ARG members worked both independently and in collaboration, in order to address each other's experiences of the intersection of diversity and business performance. ARG members had the benefit of facilitation and guidance from experts from different disciplines in order to better understand some of the 'real world' challenges of diversity. Their experiences were observed and informed by the academic research team and business consultants, and the generic lessons learned in the process are described in this report.

The research focused on four contemporary diversity management themes and their interplay with business performance, in order to reflect the needs of the group as a whole. These themes have general relevance across all economic sectors and organisations:

❖ Communicating diversity messages to bring about change.

❖ Strategic development: making diversity an integral part of, and contributor to, the business strategy.

❖ Getting started and quick wins.

❖ The representation of women at senior levels.

With the help and support of the academic research team and business consultants each ARG member identified a practical diversity challenge they faced in their own organisation. Each undertook to develop a research question related to the challenge, to concentrate their efforts on resolving this issue, sharing what they found and explaining how this might help others to make progress.

For example, the Department for Trade and Industry rightly promotes the importance of a diverse UK workforce. Recently, Mulholland, Özbilgin and Worman (2005), argued that diversity brings both positive benefits and negative implications, and that only concerted management effort can deliver positive outcomes and reduce negative ones. Furthermore, Anderson and Metcalf (2003), suggest that the 'business case argument' is not yet robust in terms of academic evidence, and that the links between diversity and business performance are yet to be universally proven.

Such conflicting views create confusion, especially for those new to the subject. Ultimately, what drives employers to act will be informed by direct experience of the business advantages, knowledge of their competitors' experience and fear of legal sanctions.

In the face of patchy evidence and increasing resistance to 'red tape' and regulation, however, new ways of convincing employers about the added value that managing diversity can bring to business performance are needed.

A new approach to diversity research might help to address a number of particular problems.

First, the interpretation of what diversity is, even among those organisations that support the notion, lacks focus. For some, diversity is equal opportunities applied to more diverse groups. For others, diversity is any individual difference that can be managed through personnel practice. Agreeing on an organisational definition of diversity and its unique dimensions and parameters, therefore, is often the first challenge for organisations to deal with.

> '...some line managers reportedly distance themselves from addressing issues out of fear of saying or doing the 'wrong' thing.'

Second, different economic sectors have different diversity objectives: while public sector organisations are often driven by their legal obligations and the promise of 'public service' delivery in their pursuit of diversity management, private sector organisations focus on business benefits, social responsibility and legal compliance. Because employers in the public, private or voluntary sectors have different emphases of interest and stakes, objectives and challenges in managing diversity, they formulate processes and policies which focus on the unique circumstances that exist in their particular economic sectors.

Third, not withstanding the above, the technical language of equal opportunities as well as its overtly 'political' stance, makes it difficult for lay practitioners to pick up the core messages and to implement relevant and appropriate organisational change initiatives.

For example, some line managers reportedly distance themselves from addressing issues out of fear of saying or doing the 'wrong' thing. This fear of treading on eggshells fosters nervousness in taking action and stops innovative, creative solutions being developed.

Fourth, communicating the value of diversity (and, therefore, justifying its importance) has proved problematic. For example,

commercial interest in diversity often lies in the bottom line. Yet it isn't always clear how diversity and competitive advantage are causally related.

Diversity management activities such as setting up new training and development programmes have real costs, but demonstrating tangible benefits in 'hard cash' terms is difficult.

Nevertheless, there are 'smart' measurement techniques that have been developed to document evidence on the business case for diversity management. Measuring success is addressed by the CIPD in a change agenda report, *Managing diversity: measuring success* (Tatli *et al*, 2006), which describes the challenges and ways of approaching measurement.

Finally, though inconclusive, the evidence about the business case for managing diversity is increasing – especially anecdotally. This needs to be presented more forcefully and more frequently to employers, to raise their awareness and improve their understanding, in order that they begin to get the message about the importance of taking action to make managing diversity a mainstream business issue.

Gender and race equality law has existed for over three decades. Yet decades later, statistics show that the gender and race diversity of senior employees has barely improved.

The continued existence of inequality, despite increasing legal provisions, was the subject of other CIPD research by Leighton (2004), in which the effectiveness of law as a driver for diversity progress was debated and the importance of education and awareness emphasised.

However, all is not doom and gloom. There are signs that more progress is being made and that some employers have embraced progressive approaches to measuring and managing the impact of diversity.

A separate study being progressed by the CIPD at the time of writing this report, will survey diversity policies and practices among UK employers in order to produce benchmarking information against which progress can be judged.

Managing diversity is still a relatively new management concept. Diversity progress will depend on a range of different drivers including committed leadership and personal commitment and understanding, as well as documented economic and moral justifications for achieving greater diversity

So how can we leverage leadership in managing diversity and encourage more people to do it, if the business case is not convincing enough?

The answer to this question lies not simply in the better articulation of facts and figures about managing diversity and the intellectual arguments in favour, (although we should still do this), but in promoting the value of *doing it* and gathering real-life evidence and experience.

There is a *Hobson's* choice for organisations today regarding managing diversity. Either, wait till more evidence is available – but this is likely to stall progress – or, get on with it and learn about diversity management by doing it! This is the basis of action research.

EXECUTIVE SUMMARY

This report of a longitudinal action research study into managing diversity shares the concerns, joy, pain and experience of a group of managers from different backgrounds and disciplines, who were brought together in a learning adventure. Representatives from nine different organisations from the public, private and voluntary sectors, worked together as a collective unit of discovery in the action research programme. The following organisations, some of which are anonymous, took part in the programme:

From the public sector

Stockport Metropolitan Borough Council
Government Department X
Government Department Y
Government Department Z

From the private sector

HBOS plc
Ford Europe
Barclays Bank plc
Tesco plc

From the voluntary sector

WRVS

The programme involved setting up an Action Research Group (ARG) made up of people with different backgrounds, perspectives and approaches, to solve and practise aspects of diversity management relevant to them and the different organisations they represented.

The ARG was facilitated and recorded by academic advisers and organisational change specialists and co-ordinated by the CIPD.

Participation was self-funded, and the greatest asset contributed was the time and enthusiasm of the nine diversity managers from the delegate organisations.

The ARG members worked both independently and in collaboration, in order to address each other's experiences of the intersection of diversity and business performance. ARG members had the benefit of facilitation and guidance from experts from different disciplines in order to better understand some of the 'real world' challenges of diversity. Their experiences were observed and informed by the academic research team and business consultants, and the generic lessons learned in the process are described in this report.

The research focused on four contemporary diversity management themes and their interplay with business performance, in order to reflect the needs of the group as a whole. These themes have general relevance across all economic sectors and organisations:

❖ Communicating diversity messages to bring about change.

❖ Strategic development: making diversity an integral part of, and contributor to, the business strategy.

❖ Getting started and quick wins.

❖ The representation of women at senior levels.

With the help and support of the academic research team and business consultants each ARG member identified a practical diversity challenge they faced in their own organisation. Each undertook to develop a research question related to the challenge, to concentrate their efforts on resolving this issue, sharing what they found and explaining how this might help others to make progress.

This report contains short summaries of the projects that were undertaken and the generic learning from them. Commercially sensitive information has not been reported, to comply with the rules for taking part.

Significant lessons were learned by everyone involved. Sometimes these were painful, sometimes inspirational, but all resulted in personal growth and gain as well as organisational benefits. While, on a personal level, those taking part have made friends and developed rewarding working relationships, the key findings have shaped the guidance in this report.

With the advantages of a group environment which valued diverse perspectives and group synergy, creativity and innovation flourished and helped to build participants' confidence and shape progress in individual projects.

The value of this kind of supported network environment in fostering a learning environment and stimulating diversity progress is clear from the results and the personal testimonies of those who took part. The experience helped to debunk myths about equality and diversity and encouraged people to focus on practical solutions relevant to their organisation's business objectives. The participants adopted roles as key change agents, to help create workplace cultures in which people feel comfortable and able to give their best.

Based on the lessons learned from the action research programme, many 'top tips', general lessons and twelve key steps to make progress, have emerged. These add to the knowledge and understanding about good practice in managing diversity, as well as providing lessons about the value of action research in identifying and progressing workable solutions.

Key points

- ❖ Diversity management is about recognising and managing individual differences, not only as static socio-demographic attributes, but also as dynamic changes in people's experiences, motivations, needs and interactions in the context of work and organisations.

- ❖ The CIPD Action Research Group (ARG) offered a programme through which diversity management was conceived as an interactive, dynamic, and situated process of learning, reflecting and doing.

- ❖ The longitudinal action research programme enabled the development of individual, group and organisational benefits of diversity management to be identified and cultivated.

INTRODUCTION

❖ **Background about the challenge of managing diversity**

❖ **Defining diversity**

❖ **Managing diversity, what the debate is about**

❖ **Why action research could add to understanding**

THE DIVERSITY CHALLENGE AND BACKGROUND TO THE CIPD ACTION RESEARCH INITIATIVE

Before we explain why action research was considered to be the best way of exploring the challenges of progressing diversity in organisations we need to pose a pivotal first question:

> Question: If you were to ask a room full of people responsible for progressing diversity in their organisations, 'What is your definition of diversity?', how many different definitions and interpretations do you think you would get?

Answer: Probably as many as the number of people in the room. And that's a fact. We know because we tried it ourselves! We invited nine people, some of whom were from organisations noted for their experience and expertise in diversity (and who were facing a strategic challenge to develop diversity within their organisations) into a room and asked that very question. The answers ranged from a version of equal opportunities covered by legislation, through to the concept of 'inclusion' – which to some *cognoscenti* in the diversity field is a preferable term, involving similar values and principles, with an added objective of not only achieving diversity, but also cohesion between workers.

This *diversity* of understanding about the subject creates the first challenge in the development of general guidance on managing diversity. The CIPD responded to this challenge in the mid 1990s by publishing a position paper on managing diversity. This contained a definition, set out business case arguments for action and recommendations for making progress. This report was replaced early in 2005 by a new CIPD guide *Managing diversity:*

people make the difference at work – but everyone is different (Worman, Bland annd Chase).

The definition of managing diversity, promoted by the Institute is inclusive.

> *Managing diversity is about valuing people as individuals, as employees, customers and clients – everyone is different.*

This definition develops the definition used by one of the most influential and well-received definitions of diversity management in the UK given by Kandola and Fullerton (1998, p7):

> *The basic concept of managing diversity accepts that the workforce consists of a diverse population of people consisting of visible and non-visible differences including factors such as sex, age, background, race, disability, personality and work style and is founded on the premise that **harnessing these differences will create a productive environment in which everyone feels valued, where all talents are fully utilised and in which organisational goals are met.***

DIVERSITY AND THE BUSINESS CASE, THE DEBATE RAGES ON

Although there is mounting evidence about the business case for managing diversity as argued in the CIPD guide on managing diversity (2005), the argument as to whether organisations should concern themselves with managing diversity at all, rages on.

For example, the Department for Trade and Industry rightly promotes the importance of a diverse UK workforce. Recently, Mulholland, Özbilgin and Worman (2005), argued that diversity brings both positive benefits and negative implications, and that only concerted management effort can deliver positive outcomes and reduce negative ones. Furthermore, Anderson and Metcalf (2003), suggest that the 'business case argument' is not yet robust in terms of academic evidence, and that the links between diversity and business performance are yet to be universally proven.

Such conflicting views create confusion, especially for those new to the subject. Ultimately, what drives employers to act will be informed by direct experience of the business advantages, knowledge of their competitors' experience and fear of legal sanctions.

In the face of patchy evidence and increasing resistance to 'red tape' and regulation, however, new ways of convincing employers about the added value that managing diversity can bring to business performance are needed.

A new approach to diversity research might help to address a number of particular problems.

First, the interpretation of what diversity is, even among those organisations that support the notion, lacks focus. For some, diversity is equal opportunities applied to more diverse groups. For others, diversity is any individual difference that can be managed through personnel practice. Agreeing on an organisational definition of diversity and its unique dimensions and parameters, therefore, is often the first challenge for organisations to deal with.

> '...some line managers reportedly distance themselves from addressing issues out of fear of saying or doing the 'wrong' thing.'

Second, different economic sectors have different diversity objectives: while public sector organisations are often driven by their legal obligations and the promise of 'public service' delivery in their pursuit of diversity management, private sector organisations focus on business benefits, social responsibility and legal compliance. Because employers in the public, private or voluntary sectors have different emphases of interest and stakes, objectives and challenges in managing diversity, they formulate processes and policies which focus on the unique circumstances that exist in their particular economic sectors.

Third, not withstanding the above, the technical language of equal opportunities as well as its overtly 'political' stance, makes it difficult for lay practitioners to pick up the core messages and to implement relevant and appropriate organisational change initiatives.

For example, some line managers reportedly distance themselves from addressing issues out of fear of saying or doing the 'wrong' thing. This fear of treading on eggshells fosters nervousness in taking action and stops innovative, creative solutions being developed.

Fourth, communicating the value of diversity (and, therefore, justifying its importance) has proved problematic. For example,

commercial interest in diversity often lies in the bottom line. Yet it isn't always clear how diversity and competitive advantage are causally related.

Diversity management activities such as setting up new training and development programmes have real costs, but demonstrating tangible benefits in 'hard cash' terms is difficult.

Nevertheless, there are 'smart' measurement techniques that have been developed to document evidence on the business case for diversity management. Measuring success is addressed by the CIPD in a change agenda report, *Managing diversity: measuring success* (Tatli *et al*, 2006), which describes the challenges and ways of approaching measurement.

Finally, though inconclusive, the evidence about the business case for managing diversity is increasing – especially anecdotally. This needs to be presented more forcefully and more frequently to employers, to raise their awareness and improve their understanding, in order that they begin to get the message about the importance of taking action to make managing diversity a mainstream business issue.

Gender and race equality law has existed for over three decades. Yet decades later, statistics show that the gender and race diversity of senior employees has barely improved.

The continued existence of inequality, despite increasing legal provisions, was the subject of other CIPD research by Leighton (2004), in which the effectiveness of law as a driver for diversity progress was debated and the importance of education and awareness emphasised.

However, all is not doom and gloom. There are signs that more progress is being made and that some employers have embraced progressive approaches to measuring and managing the impact of diversity.

A separate study being progressed by the CIPD at the time of writing this report, will survey diversity policies and practices among UK employers in order to produce benchmarking information against which progress can be judged.

Managing diversity is still a relatively new management concept. Diversity progress will depend on a range of different drivers including committed leadership and personal commitment and understanding, as well as documented economic and moral justifications for achieving greater diversity.

So how can we leverage leadership in managing diversity and encourage more people to do it, if the business case is not convincing enough?

The answer to this question lies not simply in the better articulation of facts and figures about managing diversity and the intellectual arguments in favour, (although we should still do this), but in promoting the value of *doing it* and gathering real-life evidence and experience.

There is a *Hobson's* choice for organisations today regarding managing diversity. Either, wait till more evidence is available – but this is likely to stall progress – or, get on with it and learn about diversity management by doing it! This is the basis of action research.

Reason and Bradbury (2001) suggest: 'There is no short answer to the question, 'What is action research?' However, they offer an introductory definition describing action research as:

> ...a participatory, democratic process concerned with developing practical knowing in the pursuit of worthwhile human purposes....

In other words, even if you don't know precisely where you are or where you are going, it is still possible to learn about the world that you live in by experiencing and reflecting on the process in a planned and open manner.

SO WHAT IS ACTION RESEARCH ALL ABOUT?

2

* **This chapter describes what action research is about**

* **Why we adapted the technique**

* **Introduces the process of co-operative action science**

* **Explains how these techniques can be used to leverage diversity management**

In the 1990s, Eden and Huxham (1996) noted that management research has moved en masse away from objective and detached research methods towards socially aware and subjective methodologies. The tide of qualitative methods (for example – Husserl's (1946) phenomenology; Glaser and Strauss's (1967), grounded theory; Reason and Rowan's (1981) 'new paradigm' inquiry; Yin's (1989) case-study method, and so on) that emerged in this era, has been driven by the failure of scientific approaches to provide effective explanation for human behaviour and interactions in their situated contexts.

Objective and detached approaches to management research, where the researcher has little or no interest in immediate implementation of the findings, have been criticised as being objectionable in terms of their lack of value to management practice.

Understanding the place of action research in this context is clear: there has been a need for developing an understanding of the world, in a way which can help shape the reality of that world in return.

> 'Action research is defined as an involved choice in which both the researcher and the participant collectively shape their own social reality.'

Easterby-Smith *et al*, (2002), present a schema that summarises the key research methodologies. Action research is defined as an involved choice in which both the researcher and the participant collectively shape their own social reality. Therefore, the artificial barrier between the participant and the researcher is removed. In the context of management research, the practitioner becomes the researcher, and vice versa.

Hence, the researcher and the practitioner develop actionable knowledge by investigating alternative methods of collecting data,

analysing such data and identifying the management implications of their analyses concerning real-life problems.

Diversity surveys are useful to identify organisational performance against diversity standards and the scope of diversity in organisations, or opinions about diversity's relevance and importance to organisations and people. But surveys are less useful when it comes to finding out specifically about the 'ins' and 'outs' of how organisations progress diversity, achieve diversity standards, overcome resistance to change, or achieve desired results.

There are also limitations with case-study research. Case studies are often perceived as mere descriptions of historical contexts that offer little insight or foresight, which is what managers need to address their own contemporary concerns.

Action research overcomes such research method limitations and develops insight and foresight by relating both to live experience, with informed and validated insights, a combination that is made possible by academic–practitioner collaboration.

The basic model of action research involves a continuous cycle of planning, acting, observing and reflecting (McNiff and Whitehead, 2002:40), that leads to a revised plan and further cycles of act, observe and reflect (see Figure 1 on page 6).

All forms of action research are based on this fundamental model, which itself has been spawned from models of experiential learning (Kolb, 1984) and management development (Honey and Mumford, 1992).

There are variations of practice and forms for action research that focus on altering the nature and importance of each element of the cycle.

The CIPD action research project was based on the premise of extensive planning and identification of core concerns in an

Figure 1   ❖   Cycles of Action Research

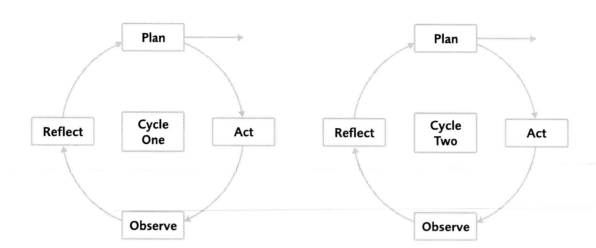

organisation, agreeing terms of reference, research parameters, measures and desirable outcomes regarding diversity.

Following the planning phase, participants acted on their individual plans and carried out their own research and implementation activities within their organisations, keeping records based on their observations in the process.

At regular intervals, the Action Research Group (ARG) met to reflect on its own and other members' research projects. This continuous learning in the action research process made it possible for group members to sharpen the focus of their research questions, to reformulate their key issues about diversity, and to arrive at more realistic diagnoses and prognoses of their diversity progress.

The above is an ideal depiction of action research. The CIPD initiative exhibited a number of problems that posed difficulties for the research team.

The problems

❖   The meaning of diversity was unclear, and there was no collective agreement.

❖   The purpose and approach to diversity differed between the economic sectors represented.

❖   Some information was confidential and sensitive.

❖   The experiences of individual group members were dissimilar.

❖   There were concerns and issues about the lack of convergence and levels of theoretical knowledge and practical experience .

To address these problems the CIPD ARG took the following steps.

Problem 1: The meaning of diversity was unclear, and there was no collective agreement

To overcome these issues the action research group went through a process of problem definition. This involved each member describing their definition of diversity and how it fitted the context in their organisation. The process helped everyone to develop their own definitions, and understand how their concerns about diversity were contextualised.

Problem 2: The purpose and approach differed across economic sectors.

The membership of the CIPD ARG included 14 co-researchers (two academics, a co-ordinator from the CIPD; two diversity business specialists; four private sector, board-level diversity champions; four public sector, senior civil servant-level diversity champions, and one not-for-profit diversity champion. The advantages stemming from this opportunity for inter-sector mentoring were the main reasons why some participants decided to take part.

The mentoring involved shadowing and sharing experiences in dyadic and triadic groups. This gave members the chance of relating to two or three different perspectives: the impact of diversity in their own organisation, the relative impact of a similar aspect of diversity in a partner organisation and the impact of diversity and generalisation of learning outcomes from the whole action research group.

This reflective practice supports the notion of territories of experience, and applies the logic of first-, second- and third-person reflections. Hence, the action research practice became three inter-connected cycles of learning – each one supporting the measurement or observation of new possibilities. In this way, different perspectives helped address problems and became a source of creative ideas through the transfer of knowledge and stimulation of innovation.

Commercial knowledge is an important aspect of competitive advantage in today's economic climate and, therefore, sensitive.

Problem 3: Some information was confidential and sensitive

Commercial knowledge is an important aspect of competitive advantage in today's economic climate and, therefore, sensitive. To stop this inhibiting the learning, all ARG members were asked to commit themselves to the 'Chatham House rule'* in their exchanges. Without such an agreement, the positive benefits of collaborative behaviour, trust and interdependence could not have been achieved. The protocol to which each member signed up made the free exchange of information possible and everyone benefited, including the research programme itself.

Problem 4: The experiences of the prospective group members were dissimilar.

The representation of different economic sectors in the make-up of the ARG added a valuable source of learning that supported the goals of sharing and reinforcing commonalities, as well as generating new knowledge through the cross-fertilisation of ideas. It turned out, in practice, to be a benefit rather than a problem of the research approach.

> 'As previous CIPD research has shown, public, private and voluntary sector organisations often take different approaches to managing diversity.'

As previous CIPD research has shown, public, private and voluntary sector organisations often take different approaches to managing diversity. It was, therefore, educational for members of the group to observe these differences first hand.

Furthermore, in terms of mentoring, the formation of dyadic and triadic mentoring relationships between participants from different economic sectors helped to dilute the competitive pressures in information exchanges. For example, whereas two participants from the same economic sector may have anticipated difficulties in being open with information they considered to be competitive, the same difficulty was not in evidence in inter-sectoral exchanges. On the contrary, the experience in the ARG was that dissimilarity between personal expertise and sectoral affiliations did not cause difficulties but created fruitful information exchanges.

Problem 5: There were concerns that theoretical knowledge and practical experience did not converge

The role of the academic researcher in a research process can distort the balance of power or, as Torbert (1991) terms it, 'power of balance'. By removing the artificial barrier between the researcher and the participants, making the power imbalances more transparent in the process, and engaging the academics and managers towards common goals, fluidity can be achieved in the transfer of knowledge between academic and practitioner .

The group cycle in the CIPD project was supported by external researchers. They facilitated action learning by offering individual mentoring and research support, through exchanges in dyadic and triadic mentoring partnerships, as well as through group feedback at quarterly meetings of the whole group.

The academic researchers offered insights and interpretations about the evidence on diversity management and its links with business performance and contributed to the individual organisations and sub-groups . And, at the group meetings, they helped to explore issues and problems raised, and to generate new questions for further investigation on an individual, partnership and group basis.

As the ARG included experienced and novice members regarding managing diversity, people were placed in separate groups to make sure the experienced members did not dominate conversations and exchanges.

The formal group meetings were managed to make sure everyone contributed and had equal discussion time with their colleagues, to talk about their individual projects and how they were progressing them.

Outside the formal group meetings, there were also self-organised, informal group meetings where novice and experienced members discussed issues together and drew on each other's expertise and experiences.

* The rule states: 'When a meeting, or part thereof, is held under the Chatham House Rule, participants are free to use the information received, but neither the identity nor the affiliation of the speaker(s), nor that of any other participant, may be revealed.' (The rule was devised in 1927 at Chatham House in London, home of the Royal Institute of International Affairs.)

HOW THE CIPD SET UP THE DIVERSITY ACTION RESEARCH PROGRAMME

3

❖ **Why the action research methodology was used**

❖ **How the action research methodology was used**

❖ **Five challenges in setting up the diversity CIPD action research initiative**

WHY ACTION RESEARCH?

Because of the limitations of various research methodologies referred to in the previous chapter, rather than in-depth case-study interviews or a large-scale survey, a technique was needed that would enable observations to be made about the conceptualisation, design, development and implementation of diversity initiatives in real-life situations.

Such a technique would reveal why employers take action on managing diversity, their views about what managing diversity is and the experiences they have in seeking to implement initiatives to make progress and add value.

To acquire this kind of qualitative research information required an innovative form of qualitative research that would help the development of insight and foresight, help to inform actions and outcomes and track progress.

The idea of an action research group on diversity developed from a conversation between the two academic members of the ARG, who were commissioned by the Institute to explore the business case for diversity and its relationship to business performance.

While discussing the overlap of interests in diversity from their respective disciplines of marketing and employment relations, they discussed the potential of involving a group of employers and diversity practitioners in a programme of research and good practice. It would be designed to help them progress diversity in their own organisations in practical ways, by making use of relevant academic knowledge and theory, and using business experience to inform what they did.

By drawing on specialist knowledge and experiences in this way, it would be possible to shape more effective ways of progressing diversity and also to observe, inform and capture how to do this in a range of contexts. The generic findings could then be published, to help others to make progress in their own circumstances, in ways that support organisational objectives and contexts.

THE CHALLENGES OF SETTING UP THE PROGRAMME

The idea for such a research programme was innovative and aspirational. Setting it up was a different matter and presented a number of challenges for the CIPD.

Challenge number one

The first challenge was to engage experts in good business practice to ensure approaches to progressing diversity were rooted in 'bottom-line' considerations.

Three consultants from Whitmuirs, with various backgrounds in change and organisation management techniques and an understanding of diversity, as well as experience of working with employers in the public, private and voluntary sectors, were recruited to be part of the support team for the research.

Challenge number two

The second challenge was to engage a small group of motivated participants from a range of organisations across different sectors of the economy.

A number of different organisations were invited to a seminar to explain to them the purpose of the research, how it would be conducted and what would be involved in taking part.

Nine organisations representing the public, private and voluntary sectors secured funding to take part in the longitudinal study, which lasted for two years. The organisations included

Private sector

❖ Barclays Bank plc

❖ HBOS plc

❖ Ford Europe

❖ Tesco plc

Public sector

❖ Government Department X

❖ Government Department Y

❖ Government Department Z

❖ Stockport Metropolitan Borough Council

Voluntary sector

❖ WRVS

Challenge number three

To create trust and confidence in sharing information relevant to learning about progressing diversity, which group members felt might be commercially sensitive, a protocol based on the 'Chatham House' rule was designed that members signed up to.

Challenge number four

To establish a firm foundation for the project, participating organisations needed a common anchor for the work they were to embark on. It was important to create united understanding about managing diversity and its relevance to business success – which was a learning process in itself. Those invited to take part in the launch seminar used different definitions and had different understandings, had different levels of expertise in diversity, and worked in different organisations with different levels of sophistication in the way diversity informed what their organisations did.

Challenge number five

The fifth challenge was to investigate what could be learned from the differences in interpretation and practice of diversity and why the different organisations involved in the programme had arrived at different points, travelled different journeys and what diverse stakeholder pressures and motivations had informed their actions. Each organisation needed a route map to help to navigate diversity progress in their own settings.

Organisations at the initial seminar formed the basis of the ARG which met and progressed research over the next two years. As described in the next chapter, each focused on a specific project and theme to help illuminate progress and highlight the business contribution.

THE CIPD ACTION RESEARCH GROUP PROJECT THEMES

4

- ❖ **How nine organisations were signed up to the CIPD diversity action research programme**

- ❖ **Embracing different levels of understanding and expertise about diversity**

- ❖ **Common project themes**

This chapter concerns the experiences and learning of a group of people from nine different organisations who signed up to the Institute's unique research initiative.

Members of the ARG undertook their own individual organisational-based projects that each one had identified as relevant to their organisation's business objectives. Over the period of the action research programme, each group member was supported by the academic and consultant team and by their contemporaries doing similar projects.

> 'Members of the ARG undertook their own individual organisational-based projects that each one had identified as relevant to their organisation's business objectives.'

Individual projects were carried out over an 18-month period and, over a period of two years members attended group meetings co-ordinated by the CIPD, to share each others' experiences and exchange ideas and suggestions, as part of a review and reflection process.

The review and reflection process was informed by the academic and consultant team and finished with a final presentation and celebratory event. The learning from this process can be read in the CIPD change agenda, *Managing diversity: learning by doing* (2005), which can be downloaded by CIPD members free of charge, from the CIPD website.

THE STARTING POINTS

For three private sector organisations represented on the ARG diversity is a strategic objective and approaches to managing diversity are well-developed and sophisticated. Each of these organisations has received some form of external recognition for the achievements they have already made.

Some of the group members from the public sector were championing diversity both as a stand-alone 'good thing' and as a strategic contributor, whilst the others were in the early stages of introducing diversity.

> 'Some of the group members from the public sector were championing diversity both as a stand-alone 'good thing' and as a strategic contributor, whilst the others were in the early stages of introducing diversity.'

In the voluntary sector, the WRVS had begun to address diversity and, for specific reasons, focused on improving business performance.

Despite this range of experience, all ARG members were able to contribute to and benefit from the group discussions about how diversity is defined, why it is important, how diversity can be leveraged to improve performance and what tools are available to manage diversity.

HOW THE PROJECTS WERE THEMED

The individual projects identified by each ARG member fell into one of the four themes illustrated in Table 1 on page 12.

To respect the issues of confidentiality and commercial sensitivity, some of the individual projects outlined below are not attributed. In these circumstances, the work done has been described in general terms, while some ARG members have contributed more detailed information about the work they undertook and agreed to be identified.

Table 1 ❖ Individual project themes	
Theme	Numbers of ARG members involved in each theme
Communicating diversity messages to bring about change.	Three
Getting started and quick wins.	Two
Strategic development.	Two
The representation of women at senior levels.	Two

Issues under the four themes shown in Table 1 were the basis of group discussions as well as individual projects. This was an important part of the review and reflection process at group level, as significant comparisons could be made about purpose and context and generic lessons drawn out about the theme topics.

Individual projects are outlined in Chapter 5 under the specified four themes.

5

THE CIPD ACTION RESEARCH PROJECTS AND OUTCOMES

❖ **The four project themes: communicating diversity messages, getting started and quick wins, strategic development and the representation of women at senior levels**

❖ **Outlines of individual projects**

❖ **Tricks to spot**

❖ **General lessons**

THEME ONE: COMMUNICATING DIVERSITY MESSAGES TO BRING ABOUT CHANGE

The HBOS communication conundrum

HBOS resulted from the merger of two very different businesses. In September 2001, Halifax, previously a building society with 40,000 employees, merged with the Bank of Scotland, employing 20,000 people. The former had a focus on personal banking and was based in Halifax, while the latter specialised in corporate and business banking, and was based in Edinburgh.

In diversity terms, both organisations had different backgrounds. Halifax was highly diverse and had supporting strategies in connection with the recruitment, selection and development of people, a high proportion of women at senior levels, and a workforce broadly representative of the national population in terms of disabilities and ethnic origin. The Bank of Scotland had a much lower representation of these diversity categories.

Faced with these differences, the new and growing HBOS needed a communication strategy to leverage progress and engage the organisation behind its serious commitment to diversity expressed in its diversity statement:

> HBOS is : '...committed to equality of opportunity in all areas of employment and business. Our colleagues are encouraged to reach their full potential regardless of their gender, marital status, parental status, sexual orientation, age, disability, race, colour, nationality, ethnic origin, religion or political affiliation. We are determined to treat all current and potential colleagues and customers fairly and with respect.'

What they did

To do this the HBOS members of the ARG reviewed the communication programmes used by Halifax and the Bank of

Scotland, to find out how successful they had been. They compared the results of employee satisfaction surveys, and this helped them to identify what had worked in the past and consider the possibility of using other communication methods.

What they found

Their research of past communication approaches showed that the Halifax had adopted a highly centralised top-down approach. The range of communication methods had been funded centrally and was wide, including staff booklets, induction and management guidelines, road shows, flyers, exhibition stands, focus groups, executive briefings and video training. Benefits had been measured in terms of culture change, increased levels of awareness and ownership, strong branding and improved external profile.

Yet the initial adoption of a centralised approach to diversity communications in HBOS proved less successful than it had been in Halifax. The newly merged company combined a diversity of organisational cultures, with a much broader spectrum of branches, and employees with more diverse backgrounds than existed in the former organisation. There were also different diversity issues for priority attention in different parts of it.

Over the course of the ARG programme, the HBOS team improved the communication strategy which had initially been adopted, to make it more effective. They did this by including de-centralised communication, driven by localised needs and funded by local budgets.

This decentralised approach added value, as it introduced more scope for local management to prioritise and focus attention on local diversity issues within the national-level framework and also fostered local-level ownership.

What they learned

Adopting a communication strategy on the basis of what seems, on face value, to have been successful in the past, is no guarantee that it will deliver results in new and different circumstances. Neither is there one single way to get diversity messages across to everyone. Through the process of review and reflection brought about by the action learning process, different ways of addressing the communication challenge emerged.

> 'Adopting a communication strategy on the basis of what seems, on face value, to have been successful in the past, is no guarantee that it will deliver results in new and different circumstances.'

Tricks to spot

❖ there are no universal 'best' approaches: tailor what works well to the circumstances

❖ be clear about the contexts and objectives you are working with

❖ understand the different stakeholder interests of those you want to influence and get them involved in designing them

❖ design a customised strategy using an appropriate blend of techniques

❖ monitor the impact

❖ modify and review what you do, to see if it is making the difference you want to make

❖ consult others and listen to what they have to say, in order to craft messages that will interest people and encourage them to take on board what you are saying

❖ analyse the outcomes of what you do, as this will provide valuable learning.

General lessons

1 There are benefits in both centralised and decentralised communication to get across messages about diversity, but an 'either/or' approach may not work well.

2 Some messages, such as complying with the law, or organisational standards, may be better coming from a central source.

3 Messages related to local circumstances or conditions will often be better originating from local sources, through a bottom-up approach, in ways that reflect local needs, circumstances and conditions.

4 Making the messages relevant helps to engage staff and deliver ownership.

5 Top management endorsement is key to gain buy-in and stimulate action.

6 You will not convince everyone overnight. Communicating messages about diversity needs to be part of an ongoing process.

Integrating diversity into policy; or 'fine words into fruitful business activity'

Government Department X

One of the national government departments that took part in the ARG has the role of promoting the importance of managing diversity to business, based on the principle that it brings 'prosperity for all'.

But, as well as promoting diversity to other organisations, it was recognised that diversity needed to inform the department's operational activities by being integrated into all policy-making, implementation, and assessment efforts.

To achieve this, the challenge faced by the ARG member from the department was to increase awareness about diversity internally, and foster ownership and engagement, so that people willingly took on diversity in their daily tasks.

The obstacles to be overcome included a low budget, and competing demands and objectives related to other high-profile initiatives that were assumed to be more relevant and important – not an unusual story in any organisation.

So how could an impact be made, with only a small budget and competing time pressures, on the people who needed to be convinced that managing diversity is an important part of their day-to-day work? The answer was not 'rocket science' and emerged from the act, review and reflection process supported by the ARG.

What they did

The idea that emerged to motivate people in different parts of this government department to incorporate aspects of diversity into the policies they wrote, was to run a competition and reward good diversity practice. This may sound banal, but it worked. It encouraged individual departments to review their diversity practices and policies, assess progress and share examples of good practice across the workplace to encourage its adoption by others – it was, in fact, leadership by example.

The design of the competition was informed by the views, ideas and needs of a range of stakeholders in the department, a process which itself helped to foster ownership and engagement through being relevant.

This important information was gleaned through a series of two-hour focus-group discussions with members drawn from a range of junior and senior management positions, as well as representatives of various employee groups.

Advanced planning and research prepared the ground for lively debate and everyone taking part was invited to contribute. Numbers in each focus group were limited to eight.

The focus group discussions were facilitated by an independent outsider and the 'Chatham House' rule was applied, to encourage open information exchange on three themes. These were specifically identified to explore and resolve the problems facing the organisation.

They were:

❖ What was meant by diversity across the organisation and were there any examples of good practice that could be shared for achieving quick wins?

❖ How should contributions to a diversity campaign be rewarded and should there be a competition?

❖ How should diversity be communicated in the future?

What they found

The focus group participants were stimulated by the opportunity to be involved in the development of an organisational communication plan for diversity and motivated by the opportunity to share ideas, and existing good practice.

Many examples were contributed and many were more progressive than were expected. Top-down support from senior civil servants, including the Minister, lent weight to the importance of the diversity message and helped to drive it to the grass-roots level.

> 'People, rather than budgets, are likely to be the driving force behind organisational change initiatives. You do not need a huge budget.'

As the predominant culture of the organisation was co-operative, it was suggested that the competition should be focused on celebrating examples of good practice, rather than ranking them against each other – great ideas and good practice rewarded, rather than best ideas sought.

A panel was set up to ensure that both the organisation's objectives and the overall principle of diversity were being met by the examples of good practice.

Every part of the organisation was given the chance to contribute one example of good practice from their own functional area. This inclusive approach meant that there were as many good examples in the celebration of diversity as there were functional areas.

These contributions were reviewed by the panel, along with the competition initiative itself. In this way, the importance of all kinds of activities to address diversity could be recognised, to illustrate the intrinsic relevance of diversity to operational practices and the ways in which it added value to processes and outcomes.

This message was both re-emphasised and put across to a wider audience too, through a celebration event held at prestigious venue.

News about the event was spread in various ways, including people telling each other about it. This personal communication channel fuelled interest and enthusiasm for attending, as well as stretching the limited budget.

Tricks to spot

❖ involve and engage different stakeholder interests and views

❖ provide examples of what has been done

❖ offer ways of helping people to talk to each other and exchange views and ideas, with independent facilitation

❖ make opportunities to profile real examples of the ways in which addressing diversity has improved an outcome of a mainstream business activity or, conversely, how failing to do so has made it less effective.

General lessons

1 People, rather than budgets, are likely to be the driving force behind organisational change initiatives. You do not need a huge budget.

2 There is great value in identifying and promoting internal examples of good practice, rather than just those of other organisations.

3 Diversity initiatives benefit from stakeholder involvement. Without such direct involvement, it is difficult to achieve buy-in for the diversity message. People need to feel it to own it.

Raising cultural awareness on a shoestring

Government Department Y

Department Y is a complex organisation with a difficult and politically sensitive public service to deliver.

It has also undergone major changes both in its business activities and employment profile over the last decade – the latter involving a changing gender mix and an increased representation of people from black and minority ethnic groups. The nature of its business requires acute awareness of cultural issues to deliver good customer service. So an appreciation of cultural issues is an important business issue for two reasons: the diversity of its customer base and the growing diversity of its workforce.

A national-level response to this business need focused on undertaking a national training programme on diversity and equality awareness, which was planned as a compulsory course for all employees.

When discussing this proposal with members of the ARG, the value of this uniform approach was questioned, not only on the basis of cost, but also on the basis of value and effectiveness.

ARG members questioned the validity and potential benefits of a nationwide awareness and induction programme, based on their own experiences. Without exception, the opinion was that rolling out a very expensive training programme was a 'sheep-dipping' exercise, and unlikely to make significant changes to employees'

beliefs, actions or commitment. In their view, a more engaging approach would require stakeholder involvement and local-level support, driven through personal enthusiasm rather than budget.

What they did

Based on this feedback from the ARG, the diversity team from this department changed tack on the project and developed an idea for running a national diversity week.

Although this seemed a simple idea to implement, the budget to make things happen was set at £3,000 which, for such a large organisation, was very low. So the main resource to deliver success was people, not money.

The diversity team, therefore, designed a strategy to achieve buy-in for the national diversity week by drawing on the goodwill, knowledge and contacts of employees themselves.

This ambitious undertaking required a multi-party engagement of employees from branch and main office equality and diversity networks as well as from mainstream functional departments and managers, and including those at senior levels.

Getting the support of senior management to seek the involvement of the whole organisation in this celebratory week was the first hurdle to overcome. Armed with this level of support, the diversity team approached the various constituencies within the organisation for help and the contribution of ideas for the week's events.

A pool of ideas came forward and resulted in the national diversity week being a great success – so much so that it was repeated.

> '...money is not the key to success, but the engagement of employees, their goodwill, personal knowledge and commitment, is.'

For example, individual employees themselves and different diversity groups agreed to resource information stands on various diversity issues ranging from religious beliefs and festivals to cuisine, from sexuality to disability, from gender to ethnicity – so that their real-life experiences could be featured and provide opportunities for discussion and information exchange and awareness-raising using the first hand knowledge and contacts with community organisations of employees themselves.

Different diversity groups and branch networks also organised local events independently, sometimes over lunch periods, using employees' ideas for raising awareness about cultural issues.

There were major contributions from networks of workers with disabilities, as well as the gay and lesbian groups in the organisation.

Further, the minority ethnic workers' network and the trade unions also provided support.

These events provided a very important lesson about the design and funding of diversity initiatives – money is not the key to

success, but the engagement of employees, their goodwill, personal knowledge and commitment, is. Employees themselves are a vital resource for progressing diversity.

Tricks to spot

❖ a lack of funding for progressing diversity is not necessarily a hindrance – it can lead to creative and innovative ideas

❖ using in-house knowledge and experience is critical

❖ engaging stakeholders is key to cultivate ownership and interest.

General lessons

1 Don't ignore individual goodwill as a resource in achieving organisational change.

2 Goodwill, in the absence of financial support, can mobilise and leverage organisational change.

3 Training is important, but there needs to be caution about adopting a 'sheep-dip' approach as a panic reaction for speeding up change.

4 Training needs to be relevant and designed to meet an identified need and purpose.

5 Although generic training may be useful to communicate basic messages about diversity, it should not be seen as the only vehicle for changing the way people or organisations behave.

6 Activities to progress diversity need to be receptive to local conditions, be based on meaningful insights into diversity management and be relevant to stakeholders to have impact.

7 Diversity awareness programmes require multi-party involvement to achieve buy-in and the support of people from different parts of an organisation.

THEME TWO: GETTING STARTED AND QUICK WINS

Changing supply to meet demand and making diversity champions out of everyone in the WRVS

The WRVS provides a range of services to help people in need, who might otherwise feel lonely and isolated. It works with other charities and organisations, local authorities and the NHS, meeting needs in communities throughout England, Scotland and Wales. Volunteers play a vital role in everything the WRVS does: well over 90,000 of them – both men and women – give up their time to help other people and to make life better in their communities. Together with WRVS employees, they deliver professional services with a personal touch.

The organisation was initially formed to help civilians during the Second World War – in evacuation, emergency feeding and providing general care and support. Since then, WRVS services have evolved, and the organisation is now a major service provider giving practical help – particularly for older people – to enable choice, independence and dignity so that people can enjoy an improved quality of life – all with the help of volunteers.

The vision statement of the WRVS makes it clear it is committed to helping build communities where diverse individuals and organisations work together in a socially inclusive society. With increasing diversity in the communities serviced by the WRVS, this created a challenge about effective service delivery.

Supported by a new vision statement about the importance of diversity, the objective of the diversity manager was to materialise the social inclusion ambitions of the organisation.

What they did

The project the WRVS brought to the ARG was about closing the diversity gap between the diversity profile of the WRVS volunteers and the communities they serve. Most volunteers were predominantly from white, privileged, middle and upper middle class backgrounds, and could be described as a 'twin-set-and-pearls' group. Whereas, the community they served was much more diverse across a wide range of socio-demographic factors.

Another challenge the project had to address was the wide geographic distribution of WRVS operations. This reduced the effectiveness of a centralised, top-down approach, especially as the branches of the organisation have quasi-autonomous status and can therefore act independently of the centre. For this reason, to achieve buy-in for diversity initiatives, a bottom-up approach was required.

To do this, the WRVS identified local champions and provided them with recognition in the WRVS press. During the course of this project, the diversity manager travelled extensively to visit the branches and explore alternative means of achieving diversity aims with branch managers and employees, through a constructive dialogue.

What they found

By doing this research, it became clear that there was a range of local initiatives aimed at closing the diversity gap. For example, one hospital facility located in a multi-ethnic area had found that the use of the facility by the local multi-ethnic community was suffering. The food provision was limited in choice. Realising this, the local management had improved their food choices in a way that catered for wider cultural tastes. This simple improvement led to the better use of the WRVS facility by the multi-ethnic users of the hospital.

The challenge of recruiting a wider base of volunteers and staff members continues. To build on the gains in service delivery described above, the WRVS identifies best branch-level practices in the successful recruitment of staff and volunteers who represent the diversity of their local communities. It promotes these successful branches as champions to the WRVS community.

This has a number of benefits. It improves the profile of diversity initiatives, helps to support their sustainability and presents an ideal example for other branches and sections of the organisation to follow.

Tricks to spot

❖ fact-finding and basic research is important to understand the situation you are dealing with

❖ the process of investigation may reveal some useful existing practices you can build on

❖ the process of talking to people in the organisation helps to build allies and engage them

❖ showing you value what people do by recognising them for their efforts

❖ profiling good practice to others helps to effect change.

General lessons

1 It makes sense to start with small wins and extend successful ways of doing things to other parts of the organisation by example, particularly in large, complex and decentralised organisations.

> 'In large and complex organisations delegation to others is essential. One diversity person or diversity department cannot make things happen without the buy-in and the engagement of others.'

2 In large and complex organisations delegation to others is essential. One diversity person or diversity department cannot make things happen without the buy-in and the engagement of others.

3 Having diversity champions helps to improve progress.

4 Getting line management on board is key to making progress.

5 Operational examples, that show the importance of considering diversity issues in daily jobs, are invaluable.

Progressing diversity through learning – it's a two-way process

A public sector body experience

There are many types of organisations operating in the public sector, and the challenges they face in addressing and progressing diversity in the way they operate are varied For many, as well as being directly involved in taking account of diversity issues in the public policy work they do, there is a need to reflect the diversity of the population the public policies apply to, in their employee profiles.

Making sure there is not a lack of connection between these areas of responsibility is a core focus of diversity progress in the public sector, and all sorts of initiatives are practised to do this. Some are complex, pervasive and process-driven. But the following is an example of how small steps can be taken to open up bigger opportunities for change, even where there is little initial buy-in or support and no budget either.

What they did

Two simple projects were designed and delivered by the diversity manager following discussions and advice from the ARG and independent research.

Designed to meet the need to change the long-standing culture and traditional ways of doing things in the organisation, the first project was about facilitating work experience for 16–18-year-old students from disadvantaged backgrounds in the immediate and neighbouring counties.

Placements were offered to a select group of students identified through charities that work with young people. Their temporary inclusion in the workforce was non-threatening to existing employees, and provided new learning experiences for the students and for the existing workforce. This personal learning was noticed, through anecdotal evidence, to have subtle but positive effects on attitudes about the kind of people who would 'fit in' to the organisation, and stimulated attitudinal change and more radical thinking.

The second project also involved young people and was the introduction of an apprenticeship programme to meet the challenges presented by recruitment difficulties. Specialist skills needed to maintain the structure of buildings and machinery were in short supply, and innovative thinking was needed to resolve this problem.

What they found

Initially, the introduction of young people from disadvantaged backgrounds was marked with difficulties.

For example, there were practical challenges about the way the students dressed for work, as they could not afford the kind of clothes other employees wore. There were also difficulties with their travel and subsistence costs until they were paid their first salary.

Faced with the need for flexibility in addressing these simple, practical issues, employees went through a useful learning experience about the rigid nature of the prevailing culture and ways of working. It encouraged them to be more open-minded about the importance of doing things in different ways, because they valued the work the young students did and found the experience of working with them personally insightful.

Although small projects like this might be regarded by some as insignificant to diversity progress, in fact they can be very useful. This is especially the case in circumstances where buy-in for more radical change to improve diversity is not possible, or where there is little or no top-level support.

The small gains that might be delivered can add up to bigger change in the longer run, just as in the circumstances described in this case study, where the success of the small project leads to it being replicated across other parts of the organisation under different titles.

For the second, small project, the diversity manager arranged for two young apprentices to join the organisation and be trained by the existing job holders, who were soon to retire. This initiative made the best use of the knowledge and skills of the existing employees who acted as mentors to the new entrants. It also provided career opportunities for two young people from disadvantaged backgrounds and built more diversity into the employee profile of the organisation.

> '...even in very traditional organisations where more radical changes may not be immediately possible, innovative thinking can...foster diversity progress by triggering positive outcomes and personal experiences, and using them as building blocks for bigger things.'

The above examples show how even in very traditional organisations where more radical changes may not be immediately possible, innovative thinking can create small initiatives to foster diversity progress by triggering positive outcomes and personal experiences, and using them as building blocks for bigger things.

Tricks to spot

❖ use small opportunities to introduce and support change

❖ focus on operational needs rather than unrelated diversity initiatives, so that success supports business performance.

General lessons

1   Providing different kinds of social encounters for employees can help to open minds and change thinking.

2   Finding creative and pragmatic solutions to organisational needs that are based on diversity thinking, helps to bring about attitudinal change.

3   Awareness of voluntary initiatives can help to support employee resourcing and be useful in building greater diversity into the workforce.

THEME THREE: STRATEGIC DEVELOPMENT

From action to strategy

Tesco plc

Tesco plc has made diversity a core element of its business strategy, but diversity has not always been part of its business language, nor part of the corporate goal. This case study illustrates how it is possible to support diversity, before a specific strategy is developed, and how strategy can support a more concerted effort towards diversity.

On its web site, Tesco plc provides a case study on recognising age:

Les Rowe, aged 78, can be found filling shelves with fresh fruit at his local Tesco store in Goldenhill, Bristol. Eager to keep busy, he has chosen to work long past the traditional retirement age. Up until a year ago he worked as a Tesco trolley man. Appreciative of the job's responsibility he notes: 'As a trolley man you are the first and the last thing a customer sees when going into the store, a good impression is vital.' Before applying for his job with Tesco he was apprehensive that his age may be a factor that counted against him when applying, but was delighted to be told 'if you can do the job, it doesn't matter what age you are'.

Source: www.tesco.com, summer 2005.

A similar example is offered in terms of recognising disability:

Robert Artiss is a grocery assistant at our Worksop store in Nottinghamshire. Despite two National Vocational Qualifications (NVQs) and many job applications, he had only been able to find temporary work until Remploy arranged for him to join the New Deal for Disabled People programme. Badly injured in a road traffic accident when he was eight years old, Robert suffered brain damage that affected his left side, but he fought back, regaining the ability to walk and carry out everyday activities. During a six-week work placement at Tesco, Robert's enthusiasm shone through, and he was eventually offered a permanent job. Delighted with his job, Robert feels that the best aspect of working at Tesco is the companionship: 'The people at Tesco are brilliant,' he says. 'My disability means nothing to them – they see the person I am inside.'

Source: www.tesco.com, summer2005.

Rice in big bags please – product diversity

As a commercial organisation, Tesco is keen to build its market share and volume, but this is difficult when the existing product range is already extensive. Asking for and using customer feedback has become a key element of Tesco's success, an example of which was one suggestion that many of the ethnic customers wished to buy rice in large amounts, not normally stocked at their local Tesco store. In trial stores, Tesco introduced larger packaged quantities of rice and found a staggering increase in sales. These sales were not just larger than existing sales, but actual value and volume increased, meaning the sales were being achieved against other suppliers.

Against the background of all this activity, the challenge for the ARG member from Tesco was to convert these activities into a strategy, so that the principles of diversity became embedded into the culture and future of the organisation.

What they did

As part of their involvement with the ARG, the Tesco representative networked with experienced diversity colleagues to learn from their experiences and develop their own knowledge and understanding. These experiences, and internal work on strategy development, helped them to merge Tesco's existing good practices on diversity into a strategic diversity plan. This was presented to the Executive at Tesco to demonstrate a business case for the inclusion of diversity into the corporate objectives.

What they found

The key to strategic diversity development was linking the core business objectives to Key Performance Indicators (KPIs), which fitted closely to the Tesco Steering Wheel management process (see Figure 2 on page 20).

Without KPIs specifically developed for diversity, it would not have been possible to include diversity in the strategic business plan.

The review of KPIs, and linking them to diversity and inclusivity is essential for diversity to succeed, because the steering wheel drives Tesco business direction throughout the management process. As explicitly stated:

We [Tesco] use one or all of the following criteria to choose our KPIs:

- *Customer priorities, for example, our KPIs on recycling, local sourcing, organics and the Computers for Schools scheme reflect our customers' concerns;*

- *Staff priorities, for example, our KPIs on training and charitable giving;*

- *Business priorities, which include financial and non-financial risks and opportunities. For example, our KPIs on supply chain labour standards and energy and water usage all are intended to help us manage the risks posed by globalisation and climate change;*

- *Compliance with legislation or public policy. For example, our KPIs on refrigerants and energy efficiency reflect the demands of current UK Government environmental initiatives.*

Source: www.tesco.com, summer 2005.

The Tesco Steering Wheel is central to successfully incorporating diversity into the culture of the business, and the Steering Wheel process allows interpretation of local diversity within local geographic stores.

Every store also has its own individual Steering Wheel, which is linked to every person's objectives, relating strategy to day-to-day work. Our international businesses, which operate locally, also have their own Steering Wheels .

(www.tesco.com).

The Steering Wheel drives the direction of the business, while recognising the constraints of the market and business stakeholders,

Each segment is driven and monitored by KPIs, which set demanding but achievable targets for the business, and are backed by a sound business case quantifying the

Figure 2 ❖ **The Steering Wheel management process**

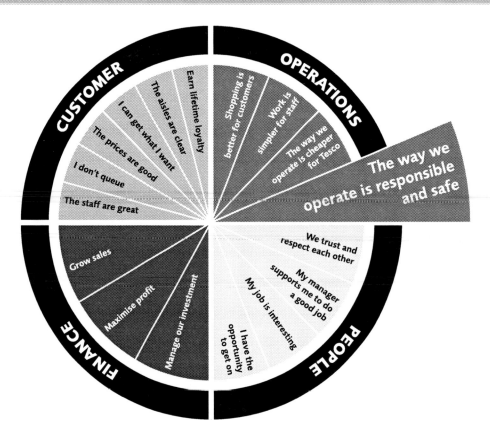

Table 2 ❖ **Tesco KPIs for 2005/06**

KPI	KPI for 2005/06
Inclusivity and diversity	No statistical difference by age, sex or ethnicity in answer to the staff Viewpoint survey question 'I look forward to coming to work'.
Healthy living	To have 2,000 products subject to new nutritional signposting. To increase the number of Healthy Living Club members from 220,000 to 500,000.
International Corporate Responsibility	To hold workshops for our International businesses. Our businesses to have a CR strategy with performance measured in their Steering Wheel.

benefits. Where KPIs are not on track, the Steering Wheel Group puts in place action plans. Performance is reported quarterly to the Board, and a summary report is sent to the top 2,000 managers in the company to cascade to staff. The remuneration of senior management is shaped by the KPIs, with bonuses based on a sliding scale according to the level of achievement on the Corporate Steering Wheel.

The implications

For 2005/06 this means that every manager now has a set of goals specifically for diversity, which means that their success and reward is linked to making diversity happen (see Table 2 above).

Tricks to spot

❖ checking out the meaning of diversity and relating this to the way the organisation does things can show where there are already pockets of good practice

❖ some working practices may already dovetail with good diversity practice, even if not labelled as such

❖ if you discover that working practices are focused on valuing the advantage of 'difference', flexibility, fairness and business ethics – then progressing diversity as a mainstream business issue will be congruent and lend weight to achieving an inclusive workforce and customer base.

General lessons

1   The integration of diversity management principles into business performance and strategy processes and systems helps to focus organisational efforts to achieve real diversity progress and systemic change.

2   For some organisations, diversity management is a strategic and competitive concern and core strategic objectives reflect diversity management philosophy.

3   Efforts to integrate diversity management principles into organisational strategy show where activities already embrace a diversity philosophy successfully and deliver added value to business performance. Such positive findings can be used as building blocks to reinforce messages about the value of thinking about diversity in mainstream business activities and make the business case for managing diversity more robust so that it becomes central to the way an organisation operates.

> 'Measuring the impact of diversity initiatives and incorporating diversity into KPIs and performance scorecards is a key method for integrating diversity successfully into business strategy and day-to-day business operations.'

4   Measuring the impact of diversity initiatives and incorporating diversity into KPIs and performance scorecards is a key method for integrating diversity successfully into business strategy and day-to-day business operations.

If you want to change it, measure it!

Ford Europe

In 1903, the same year Henry Ford founded the Ford Motor Company in the United States, two Ford Model A cars were shipped from Detroit to Britain.

Even Henry Ford could not have imagined what the next 100 years would bring for his company, or just how far-reaching its impact would be on the social, cultural and economic framework of Britain. It soon became apparent that larger premises were needed, and Henry Ford decided to establish the first Ford factory outside North America. In 1911 Percival Perry, who had taken over the Ford UK sales agency, acquired and converted a disused tram works just south of Manchester at Trafford Park and production began on October 11, 1911. Shaftesbury Avenue became the company showroom and the Ford Motor Company (England) Limited came into being. In 2003 Ford Britain celebrated the 100th Anniversary of Ford Motor Company.

The company has given its name to an '-ism' in management literature, Fordism, which denotes the mass production approaches that Ford Motor company tradition has stood for. Fordism rests uneasily with the concept of diversity because, while the former relies on a standardised approach, the latter aspires to recognise and welcome 'difference'. As diversity management at Ford is presently considered a strategic management issue, this signals the emergence of 'post-Fordism', characterised by the recognition of difference and diversity, and the use of flexible approaches in accommodating these.

> '...Fordism...denotes the mass production approaches that Ford Motor Company tradition has stood for...[and]...rests uneasily with the concept of diversity...'

Within the last decade, Ford Europe has become one of the most dedicated private companies to a diversity agenda in the UK. At the origin of Ford's success in the area of diversity management lies the robustness of the mechanisms for measuring and monitoring the impacts of diversity management.

At Ford, diversity has been integrated into all areas of business activity in all functions and is a key objective in the Balanced Scorecard of the European Board for all functional areas and line management across the organisation. In Britain, this includes the delivery and implementation of the diversity plans for each site and function. Diversity is measured against six areas of business activity: policy and planning; selection; developing and retaining staff; communication and corporate image; corporate citizenship; and auditing for diversity and equality.

The clarity of the measurement of diversity objectives and goals to deliver the diversity strategy contributes to the company's success in this field. Ford is a very systematic, process-driven company. Process drives change, and processes include clearly outlined line-management responsibility, what needs to be done on a step-by-step basis and how to measure that change.

What they did

As a member of the ARG, the Ford representative shared information and experience about managing diversity, the challenges and how to make progress, and used feedback and involvement in the group to inform the development of diversity training.

A comprehensive diversity training programme has been designed by Ford of Britain to raise the diversity awareness of the employees and managers at all levels, and involvement in the ARG helped to inform this. The training focuses on inclusion and aims to encourage employees to relate what they learn to their jobs and the way they behave at work.

The programme is themed to address job competencies and the framework includes four levels :

1   'acquiring the basic knowledge' for the employees who have just started and who do not manage anybody;

2   'applying the knowledge' for the supervisors or managers who just manage one person;

3   'guiding the people who apply the knowledge' for the team leaders and line managers, and finally,

4   'creating the knowledge' for investigators and HR professionals.

The company aims to train everybody by 2008. Everyone has to attend a one-day Diversity Awareness Workshop and Dignity at Work training.

In addition, team leaders and line managers attend a more in-depth two-day workshop on diversity. Lastly, there is a two-day programme on harassment and bullying and diversity for those responsible for investigating complaints and a three-day programme on recruitment, retention and diversity for the HR professionals.

Tricks to spot

❖ you may know more than you think but there is always something new to learn about managing diversity; never think you know it all, because it is about managing dynamic change

❖ networking and sharing information can build knowledge and confidence

❖ keeping in touch with external developments is important to inform and shape good practice

❖ customising training to different business and employee needs should be central.

General lessons

1 A systematic, process-driven approach to the management of diversity attached to core organisational values and objectives is important, in order to expedite change and make diversity a mainstream business issue, rather than an add-on activity.

2 Aligning organisational values with those of diversity management can help the organisation to reassess its stance on diversity.

3 Measurement is vital to show how and what progress is made, what got in the way and how problems can be overcome in the future.

4 In process-driven manufacturing firms, what gets measured gets done. Measurement can help organisations to drive change, if the techniques used are designed to suit the particular circumstances and contexts.

THEME FOUR: THE REPRESENTATION OF WOMEN AT SENIOR LEVELS

A view from the top

Barclays Bank plc

Barclays is a leader in the diversity field, with a host of awards and accolades for its diversity initiatives.

Its diversity programme is driven by its 'success through inclusion' values (see Figure 3, below), which have support at the very

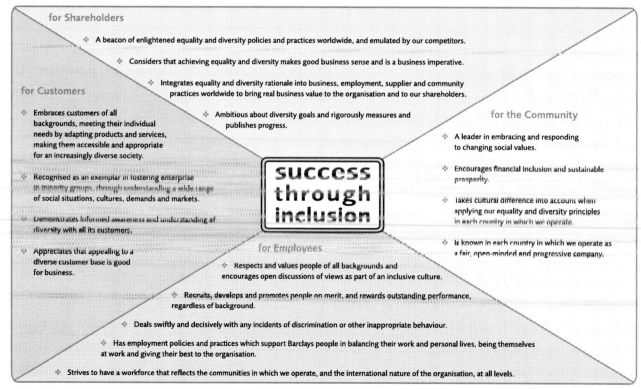

Figure 3 ❖ Barclays' Vision for Equality and Diversity

for Shareholders

❖ A beacon of enlightened equality and diversity policies and practices worldwide, and emulated by our competitors.

❖ Considers that achieving equality and diversity makes good business sense and is a business imperative.

❖ Integrates equality and diversity rationale into business, employment, supplier and community practices worldwide to bring real business value to the organisation and to our shareholders.

for Customers

❖ Embraces customers of all backgrounds, meeting their individual needs by adapting products and services, making them accessible and appropriate for an increasingly diverse society.

❖ Recognised as an exemplar in fostering enterprise in minority groups, through understanding a wide range of social situations, cultures, demands and markets.

❖ Demonstrates informed awareness and understanding of diversity with all its customers.

❖ Appreciates that appealing to a diverse customer base is good for business.

❖ Ambitious about diversity goals and rigorously measures and publishes progress.

success through inclusion

for Employees

❖ Respects and values people of all backgrounds and encourages open discussions of views as part of an inclusive culture.

❖ Recruits, develops and promotes people on merit, and rewards outstanding performance, regardless of background.

❖ Deals swiftly and decisively with any incidents of discrimination or other inappropriate behaviour.

❖ Has employment policies and practices which support Barclays people in balancing their work and personal lives, being themselves at work and giving their best to the organisation.

❖ Strives to have a workforce that reflects the communities in which we operate, and the international nature of the organisation, at all levels.

for the Community

❖ A leader in embracing and responding to changing social values.

❖ Encourages financial inclusion and sustainable prosperity.

❖ Takes cultural difference into account when applying our equality and diversity principles in each country in which we operate.

❖ Is known in each country in which we operate as a fair, open-minded and progressive company.

Source: www.barclays.com, summer 2005.

highest levels, and is integrated into the core business indicators. This in turn is co-ordinated and managed through the Global Diversity Council, providing senior level governance and direction to both group and business areas.

Barclays has explicitly stated its intention to lead the world in diversity practice, to be 'a beacon of enlightened equality and diversity policies and practices worldwide' and that it will integrate 'equality and diversity rationale into business, employment, supplier and community practices worldwide'. To reinforce this commitment, the organisation has posted many of its diversity aims in the public domain.

> '...despite all efforts and explicit top-down support, the number of women at the highest levels had not increased to the levels intended.'

One aim relates to the representation of women at very senior levels. Even though there has been a significant improvement in the number of women at senior levels in the organisation, progress is slow. Other internal research into the skills of senior women as a group, showed differences compared to those of their male counterparts at the same level. To address this situation, serious attention is now given to the development of senior women. Yet despite all efforts and explicit top-down support, the number of women at the highest levels had not increased to the levels intended.

Related to this, the challenge for the ARG member from Barclays was to explore the issues further to see if the puzzle of what is holding senior women back from achieving the most influential positions in the organisation could be solved. This is a puzzle for many organisations seeking to progress diversity and, so far, no easy answers have been found.

What they did

Barclays' top ten executives, were approached and interviewed, either personally or by telephone, to find out their thoughts, ideas, observations and insights into what was holding up the progress of senior-level women to top positions.

Specific questions were posed relating to the business case for diversity, organisational culture, the rate of progress in improving the representation of senior-level women, and personal impressions of senior women as managers.

What they found

There was an overwhelming recognition that there was a business case for better gender diversity at board level, but a pervasive value that personal merit had to be the basis for all appointments, ie everyone had to prove themselves, including the men. More significantly, the general belief was that, even if there was not a business case for gender diversity, it was morally right that there should be more women working at the top level. It was seen as the 'right thing to do'.

There was no evidence of personal opinions that the performance of senior women in top jobs was less robust; in fact, often the

opposite view was held. Yet this positive climate of support had not stimulated a significant change in the gender profile at the very top of the organisation – even though it would not appear from the evidence collected to be an overt block to progress.

The general findings of the Barclays research supported other studies that had been undertaken into the reasons for the gender differences at senior levels. But the underlying causes remain an enigma. They are sometimes attributed to differences in 'self-promotion' between men and women. Put simply, men are thought to self-promote more then women, and this might contribute to the top positions in organisations remaining stubbornly male.

Wider research undertaken outside this internal study, into the under-representation of women at the very top of organisations, is also inconclusive. The internal research into top-team views and attitudes in the bank was an important step in trying to understand the situation and what was causing it, in order to decide what interventions the organisation might consider to speed up change. A focus on personal development and mentoring to support senior women was reinforced by the results.

This includes both external and internal mentoring.

Mentoring by senior colleagues is used more generally in the bank to support the development of people including those from disadvantaged backgrounds.

Mentoring helps mentors as well as mentees, and improves the way in which employees at different levels understand each other and the challenges of working in different functional areas and at different levels.

As part of their personal development, Barclays' staff are often placed on mentoring initiatives with the Prince's Trust and other charities, to offer both business and personal mentoring to members of their communities.

> '...it can be dangerous to assume you know what the problem is, just because it is common in other organisations...'

Tricks to spot

❖ talking to stakeholders helps to establish the nature of perceived obstacles and helps to get the facts you need to understand the nature of the problem you are trying to address

❖ ignoring the top-team views as stakeholders is a mistake; you need to find ways of engaging with them that are comfortable and non-threatening – good relationship management is key to gain confidence

❖ it can be dangerous to assume you know what the problem is, just because it is common in other organisations

❖ when you are working under time pressures, it can be tempting to cut corners by adopting approaches that other organisations have used in similar circumstances, without making sure they are relevant and tailoring them to your organisation's particular circumstances.

General lessons

1   Addressing how well an organisation is doing on the broad diversity front, is complex and challenging. To make progress it can be helpful to look independently at specific issues, such as gender or disability. This helps gradually to build the bigger picture as part of a wider diversity strategy and ongoing learning process, where the lessons learned can help to inform understanding of wider issues such as flexible working, access to training and development and reward, for example.

> 'Pioneering activities on diversity management can position organisations as leaders and 'early adopters' in the field and enhance corporate branding and image.'

2   Pioneering activities on diversity management can position organisations as leaders and 'early adopters' in the field and enhance corporate branding and image. As various published CIPD research evidence shows (*Managing diversity: people make the difference at work – but everyone is different*), the spin-off benefits of this can contribute to improvements in attracting and retaining talent and customers, and thereby help to enhance business performance.

3   Tracking diversity progress measurement is key. There are many different ways of doing this, including target setting. A range of measures and performance indicators will help to provide evidence of what interventions work and add value. An absence of goals and targets will reduce the ability to show the impact of diversity efforts and make them vulnerable and potentially less sustainable. The CIPD report *Managing diversity: measuring success,* gives guidance on the importance of measurement.

4   Separate CIPD research on the representation of women at senior levels (*Women in the board room: a bird's eye view*, 2004*)*, discusses the reasons why women de-select themselves from top-level positions.

Senior women and career progression

Stockport Metropolitan Borough Council

More than 291,000 people live in this borough, while many more look to Stockport for employment or entertainment. With a net annual revenue budget of £284 million in 2003/04, it provides jobs for approximately 11,000 full- and part-time employees.

The Council is both a major organisation and the biggest employer in the borough. Stockport MBC is committed to ensuring that the borough's residents and those who work in the borough have an equal opportunity to access council services.

The Council recognises the value of the diversity of its population and the richness this brings to the borough's culture. Diversity is seen in a broad context in Stockport. Not only does it mean addressing issues of race, gender, disability, but, in addition, faith, sexuality, age and, of course, poverty. The Council is working hard to root out unfair discrimination and ensure that its services are accessible to everyone.

www.stockport.gov.uk, summer 2005

One of the achievements stemming from this objective is a high representation of women in senior management positions, with an executive board typically split 50:50 between men and women.

However, it is also true that the turnover rate of senior women is higher than that of senior men and this poses a concern. Although the diversity and equality policy is robust, its success is frustrated by the loss of senior women to other employers, as illustrated by the following quotes from a Stockport MBC management report.

> *...when length of service is reviewed women have shorter service, an average of 11 years against 15 for men'.*

And

> *...from the information available, women tend to move on to other roles, while men leave as a result of retirement, or ill health.*

The challenge for the ARG member from the Stockport MBC was to consider how gender influences career progression in the organisation.

What they did

To investigate this phenomenon, the academic researchers supporting the ARG were commissioned to carry out interviews with senior men and women in the organisation to find out how they had progressed their careers and what factors they believed had helped or hindered them. Specifically, the interviews looked at

❖   what internal organisational factors either motivated or demotivated employees (senior women), and

❖   what personal factors influenced progress in either negative or positive ways

The study undertaken was based on a semi-structured telephone questionnaire, which collected five sets of data relating to

❖   the interviewee's basic details (age, management grade and employment history)

❖   personal ambitions – fears and fancies

❖   level of career development support

❖   frustrations with the organisation

❖   expectations about the future.

What they found

The strong equality and diversity culture had contributed to positive feelings among all employees. However, flexible working practices and maternity leave had fuelled perceptions about women being less committed and thereby tended to marginalise women in the career stakes.

The Council was seen as a good employer, where gender was typically not a barrier. Men tended to see the organisation as a meritocracy, where long service and career security were key features. Women on the other hand tended to cite specialist career paths as a barrier to progression. In many cases, women had put their careers 'on hold' at some point to manage parental responsibility. This, coupled with the need for improved career development opportunities for women, were the major differences between the career progression of women and men. Even so, when women rejoined senior management teams they progressed quickly, but usually had to catch up from the points they had reached before, disrupting the focus on their careers by being seen, in effect, to 'take time out' from them.

Nevertheless, this does not appear to be the full story, as indicated by the following quote from a review of turnover within The Leadership Forum (TLF):

> *Over the previous five years 60 per cent of appointments had been external, and 60 per cent female. Around 60 per cent of the cohort had less that five years' service in the role. A review of internal promotions to TLF showed a success rate of 56 per cent for women and 37 per cent for men, indicating that diversity policies at Stockport MBC had delivered high-quality employees to senior positions irrespective of gender, and that during this five-year cycle senior women had dominated the progression.*

The research commissioned by the Council showed clear psychological and sociological differences between the general patterns of behaviour and self-perceptions of men and women, which are found in other organisations, too.

'[Men]...followed the norm in terms of...their career development – typically 'having a stab' at the next promotion...to show they were 'up for it'...Women were generally more likely to be reserved in putting themselves forward...'

For example, it was clear that men held well-defined group identities with their male colleagues and followed the norm in terms of the ways in which they thought about and took action regarding their career development – typically 'having a stab' at the next promotion opportunity to show they were 'up for it' and 'interested.' Women were generally more likely to be reserved in putting themselves forward, and concerned about not being in the running unless their career experiences ticked all the right boxes regarding the needs at the next level up on the career ladder. This self-perception tended to result in women under-valuing themselves in comparison to their male counterparts.

In the same way as found in the Barclays case study, this situation focused attention on the importance of personal mentors and role models to support career development as part of the process of encouraging and developing men and women across the organisation.

Tricks to spot

❖ be on the look out for 'icebergs' – where superficial evidence, such as numbers, suggest things are ok on the surface – problems may lurk below the waterline and be bigger than you think

❖ make sure you take heed of warnings, even if they are not supported by statistical information, and aim to expose underlying issues, so you can navigate your way to success

❖ to steer the best course for progress you need to know the territory you are operating in, so fact-finding is essential to help you map out the issues you need to attend to and plan a route through the problems – second guessing could send you on a wild goose chase.

General lessons

1 Diversity management does not stop with increasing workforce diversity and the achievement of numerical recruitment targets, but must focus on retaining and continually supporting diversity, too, involving the use of qualitative, as well as quantitative, information.

2 The maintenance and sustainability of diversity needs to be part of dynamic employment systems, which focus on diversity issues in relation to participation in all aspects of employment, for example, in staff training and retention, review and turnover rates and exit interview information, flexible working and the work–life balance agenda.

3 Regarding training and development at senior levels, (as illustrated by the findings in both case studies in this ARG research), the need for varied and 'untypical' career paths to be taken into account in promotion and progression decisions, must be on the resourcing agenda, and recognition given to different ways of acquiring general management and specialist skills. Time served is not the only way to demonstrate or achieve competence.

RECOMMENDATIONS ON PROGRESSING DIVERSITY

6

❖ **Change is what progressing diversity is all about**

❖ **To be successful, change has to be appropriately managed**

❖ **The changes to be made need to be relevant**

❖ **There is no gain without pain, but ownership and engagement smooth the process of implementation through 'buy-in'**

❖ **Follow the 12 steps to success**

IT'S NOT EASY, BUT IT'S NOT ROCKET SCIENCE, EITHER

What was clear from this ARG initiative was that the management of diversity involves the management of change.

The experiences of ten people from diverse and different-sized organisations, across different economic sectors and with different levels of expertise in managing diversity, who took part in the CIPD action research initiative, have helped to build a greater understanding of some of the many challenges faced by organisations in driving progress.

All the initiatives described in this report involved making changes to the ways in which things were done. They were based on fact finding and background research and discussions with identified stakeholders, to improve understanding about the issues and determine customised solutions. This process of research and preparation enabled relationship building and the identification of change champions to help with the implementation phases and foster engagement and ownership – a process which helps to mitigate fear and resistance.

'Simply increasing workforce diversity statistics will not automatically lead to added value in terms of improved business performance.'

No matter in which economic sector organisations operate, it is clear that diversity needs to be managed to gain organisational benefits. Simply increasing workforce diversity statistics will not automatically lead to added value in terms of improved business performance.

While some organisations are well down the road towards managing diversity effectively in the workplace, others have yet to take their first steps. But, as the case studies in this report show, there are fundamental business reasons for ensuring that organisations address diversity and learn to manage it more effectively. Even those organisations at the leading edge of good practice do not have all the answers, and need to continue learning how to keep the momentum of progress going.

In driving diversity progress, employees and employers are faced with a spectrum of challenges that include the need to influence the way everyone in the organisation thinks about diversity, and to change inappropriate policies and working practices.

'Often, the changes that are needed can create uncertainty and fear, as well as new and rewarding opportunities.'

Often, the changes that are needed can create uncertainty and fear, as well as new and rewarding opportunities. The process of change can involve conflicts, stresses and strains and unintended consequences, if not appropriately managed. Both learning about and becoming proficient at managing change is, therefore, imperative for organisations seeking to make progress in managing diversity.

An earlier CIPD report addressed change management issues related to managing diversity and was based on the experiences of the ARG, published in *Managing diversity: learning by doing*, (Thomas Taylor *et al*, 2005). The learning and recommendations in

this report also dovetail with those in *HR: making change happen*, (Molloy and Whittington, 2005), which was a similar longitudinal study among nine different organisations, looking at a whole range of major organisational change and restructuring initiatives. Many of the findings were identical. For example, on the importance of involving senior managers and affected staff.

Based on the findings in this ARG diversity study, and despite the variety of circumstances faced and issues addressed, the group drew out 12 common lessons from the experiences which should be of use to any organisation looking to make further progress.

1 Business strategy should incorporate diversity management

In order for diversity management efforts to be effective and long-lived, they should be integrated into the business strategy and core values of the organisations.

Having a diversity strategy is not a pre-requisite to getting started. However, without explicit objectives, and some form of plan, driving diversity progress is likely to be difficult.

To be sustainable, diversity initiatives need to be linked to organisational goals and objectives – this makes them robust and systemic.

Piecemeal efforts that are conceived as 'add-ons' to the real work an organisation does, can be cosmetic and vulnerable and may fuel resistance if they fail to have an impact. They are less likely to do this if they are relevant to mainstream activities.

2 Diversity and the importance of measurement

To manage diversity you need to embrace the concept of measurement in some way, to show the impact of diversity initiatives.

There are many different approaches to measurement, ranging from the use of targets to the achievement of diversity standards, the use of Key Performance Indicators and of a diversity balanced scorecard.

Organisations also develop their own measurement techniques and tools, using customised indicators to track diversity in different functional areas, from finance to marketing and from sales to human resource management.

The CIPD has published a separate report giving observations and thoughts about measurement called *Managing diversity: measuring success.* (Tatli *et al*, 2006) Also, in a further report called *Managing diversity: linking theory and practice to business performance* (Mulholland *et al*, 2005), the use of a diversity balanced score card is recommended and illustrated.

3 Managing is about actions not words

A plan is critical if the diversity agenda is to metamorphose from a policy into activities related to core business issues. But plans have to be transformed into actions through the delineation of clear

application of roles and responsibilities, and with activities focused on the delivery of outcomes which should then be monitored and reviewed for effectiveness.

The implementation process can be complex. It should involve and engage all stakeholders and generally mobilise local and central resources, to ensure managing diversity becomes coherently delivered throughout an organisation.

> 'Implementation is essentially a political activity in organisational settings, through which power relationships between stakeholders often need to be renegotiated.'

Implementation is essentially a political activity in organisational settings, through which power relationships between stakeholders often need to be renegotiated. The implementation process must, therefore, be carried out with appropriate sensitivity to internal political issues and focus on transforming these power dynamics into more democratic forms which value difference.

4 Diversity champions lead the way

There are people in every organisation who have taken up the challenge of diversity themselves – for one reason or another – sometimes as part of their functional role or sometimes on a voluntary basis, because of their personal affiliations and affinities and/or beliefs in the social and economic case for diversity.

It is worthwhile identifying, developing and supporting change agents in order to progress diversity initiatives. They can bring vital energy, focus and personal resource to diversity leadership by acting as diversity champions.

5 Senior manager support is the best lever for change

Senior management support is key to any successful diversity and change management initiatives, as it opens doors for change.

Even if the top management team is not visibly diverse, it is likely that some members may support diversity management for personal reasons, or because they accept there is a business case, or because they believe it is morally the right thing to do.

Experience shows that top-down support helps to speed up change. It creates the right climate for managing diversity to 'take-off' and become an objective for the whole organisation, rather than a marginalised issue exclusively for the personnel function.

6 Engagement and ownership are essential

Valuing difference is the central component of diversity management. All individuals are unique, and everyone in an organisation has to work at recognising and becoming comfortable with difference. For diversity to progress, all employees need to understand what managing diversity is about

and be clear about their personal roles and responsibilities for supporting progress. Senior management support is vital, but effective diversity management cannot be imposed totally from above. As well as knowing their individual rights and entitlements to be treated fairly themselves, employees need to understand that their behaviour towards others needs to uphold the same values. They all need to understand and experience the benefit of diversity.

> 'Valuing difference is the central component of diversity management. All individuals are unique, and everyone in an organisation has to work at recognising and becoming comfortable with difference.'

This is where the important issue of communication comes in.

7 Communicating diversity messages results in people 'walking the talk'

Telling is not selling.

In order to persuade colleagues of the importance of managing diversity, it is essential to listen to them first and understand where they are coming from on the diversity agenda. By doing this, more effective messages can be crafted to influence thinking and effect change.

In some organisations, a centralised diversity message, which supports business goals, is a useful and effective way of getting people on board. For other organisations, a de-centralised approach is better, as it enables different parts of the organisation to create their own messages to suit local needs. In other circumstances, a blend of approaches may be preferable.

A diverse range of communication methods and channels should be considered to get messages across. For example, intranets, diversity networks and affinity groups, and special events as well as communication channels such as internal newsletters and bulletins. The aim should be to highlight examples of good practice and encourage contributions, to profile, stimulate and reinforce interest and activity.

8 Recognition and reward for diversity achievements reinforces positive behaviours

It is important to recognise and reward achievements in progressing diversity, in the same way as, for example, sales targets are rewarded.

> 'It is important to recognise and reward achievements in progressing diversity, in the same way as, for example, sales targets are rewarded.'

Recognising team efforts is as important as recognising individual efforts. Team-based initiatives can be influential in changing cultures, help to encourage engagement and ownership and lead to lasting results.

9 Ignoring diversity management is for dinosaurs

Increasingly, evidence shows how important it is for organisations to develop skills in managing diversity. Legal requirements are also increasing all the time. So, if you put off getting to grips with it, you could be jeopardising your organisation's future survival and success.

For example, the business you are in could be losing customers to more diversity-aware competitors. You could be missing out on the talent you need to employers who are well down the line at being 'employers of choice', by promoting themselves as diversity aware. Doing nothing is not a good idea, as the competition in terms of diversity management practice is already a significant reality in today's business world.

Other CIPD research demonstrates that diversity management fosters creativity and innovation, which are essential to organisations for growth and survival.

For competitive organisations, success means exceeding the expectations of customers and clients to keep ahead of competitors' offerings. Such performance requires creative and innovative approaches to business challenges and business problems. In the public and voluntary sectors, the pressures to recruit and retain a talented and diverse workforce are, if anything, even greater, as is the need to ensure a consistency between the way the public is served and the way employees are managed.

Diversity management has a role to play in achieving this, as it fosters flexible ways of thinking and working. It can help to overcome problems of organisational rigidity and inertia, by bringing new and different perspectives to solving problems, and generating ideas for taking advantage of opportunities. It can help realise new, dynamic, effective and responsive ways of doing things in different ways.

Learning about managing diversity will help your organisation to evolve and survive more effectively in today's competitive marketplace, rather than becoming extinct by being out of touch with the times.

10 Managing diversity must reflect contexts and circumstances

Not understanding the contexts and circumstances your organisation is operating in means your chances of designing diversity interventions that will support the success of your organisation are considerably reduced, and you could end up wasting efforts and resources and experiencing frustration.

Every organisation has a different trajectory and context. It is, therefore, essential that diversity management captures this unique context and that the diversity agenda is unique to the organisation's own circumstances and aims.

People commit to diversity issues that they can understand and relate to. As diversity is about valuing difference, so diversity management should reflect differences in contexts and circumstances. The evidence in this report shows that initiatives are more successful when they do.

> 'People commit to diversity issues that they can understand and relate to.'

11 Managing diversity needs patience and tenacity, but patience should not drift into inertia

Whilst getting started and keeping things going is critical, being patient is also important. Diversity management interventions will not lead to overnight success.

As in all change initiatives, adjustments and modifications may need to be made to overcome emerging and unforeseen difficulties and resistance, as progress is underway. Change needs time to evolve.

To deliver success, diversity management should include long- as well as short-term objectives. The temptation to depend totally on quick fixes could result in progress being fragile. But monitoring and measurement are critical to ensure momentum is not lost over a longer time period.

12 Progressing diversity is about continuous learning and requires change management expertise

As explained in the previous chapter, diversity management is about change management and expertise in this area is essential to changing attitudes, behaviour, culture and working practices, policies and systems.

> 'Both diversity and wide change management processes involve continuous learning – "learning by doing" – as actions taken need to be reviewed and modified to ensure they are effective.'

Both diversity and wide change management processes involve continuous learning – 'learning by doing' – as actions taken need to be reviewed and modified to ensure they are effective.

The process provides learning for individuals and the organisation and requires perseverance and reflexivity. It is important to plan and prepare for success but anticipate and face up to failure. Using mistakes and failures as learning opportunities helps to improve behaviours, actions and strategies and make them more robust and sustainable. It is unrealistic to expect to get things right from the outset, but important to remember two crucial things. One: you can't get to second base with your foot on first, and two: nobody knows everything about managing diversity.

It is important to follow the rules of effective change management to manage diversity. Nothing significant will happen unless people themselves are engaged in the actions and buy into the values that inform them.

CONCLUSIONS AND TOP TIPS FOR PROGRESS **7**

❖ **Getting started is better than doing nothing**

❖ **Learning by doing is the way forward**

❖ **Managing diversity is not just increasing diversity**

A number of useful lessons about progressing diversity came out of the ARG programme.

Using action research methods, it was possible to observe and support people learning about diversity and managing wide-ranging and complex issues in progressing it in their organisations.

The learning outcomes of the Action Research Group had far-reaching implications, both for the individuals involved in the ARG and the organisations they worked in.

The action research process helped those taking part to develop important insights into how to move initiatives forward in their organisations. They used creative problem-solving based on a reflect, think, plan and act cycle, and

❖ carried out internal fact finding and external research

❖ conducted stakeholder analysis

❖ identified opportunities and constraints

❖ built understanding of power relationships

❖ carefully designed implementation plans

❖ ensured the cross-fertilisation of ideas from people with different expertise and experiences in diversity

❖ benefited from external facilitation.

Learning by doing was central to the ARG programme and that is exactly what all organisations need to do to make progress. An earlier report, *Managing diversity: learning by doing* (Tatli *et al*, 2005), outlines the learning journey of the action research process that any organisation can follow.

AND FINALLY...

The ARG introduced a new way of thinking about diversity management and addressing diversity concerns. Everyone who took part in this important CIPD initiative went through a roller-coaster of experiences and challenges over a period of two years. But all of the business specialists, academics and practitioners involved brought different expertise and perspectives to the table and gained, on a personal level, as well as benefiting the organisations they represented.

It was a learning experience for everyone involved, resulting in a range of significant examples of successful diversity management that it is hoped will help to inform and encourage others on the diversity progress trail.

Research evidence shows that managing diversity has to be a complex, systemic, ongoing process that needs to be integrated into the way organisations function. It never has an end point.

Neither does the journey have a specific road map that all businesses can follow. However, as you step forward on the journey to progressing diversity, the report's recommendations should help you to develop specific strategies and initiatives to deal appropriately with embedding the management of diversity into business practices in your own context.

Perhaps the most valuable lesson from all the research done to date is that, to be successful, organisations need to become better at managing diversity, rather than simply improving how diverse they are.

To manage diversity successfully means challenging traditional forms of management that are based on homogeneity and ignoring difference. But times are changing and difference needs to be grappled with in organisations, because difference is the reality of our contemporary world.

Top tips for progressing diversity derived from the research

* Get started now: if you delay you may miss the boat.

* Have a strategy, but don't let not having one stop you from getting started, or responding flexibly to change.

* Check out good practice and network with others responsible for driving diversity in their organisations, but don't just copy-cat what others do – customise it to meet your organisation's needs.

* Raise awareness about the importance of managing diversity to your business, the people working for it and its customers and clients.

* Get top management backing at the earliest opportunity – find the story, evidence and arguments that will get them on board.

* Measure what you do to show how it is making a difference.

* Make diversity everyone's concern by applying diversity objectives in performance-management systems.

* Identify internal champions to help you make progress.

* Keep the messages about diversity rolling out and share learning across your organisation to motivate interest.

* Listen to stakeholders, collect their views and experiences, so that you are tuned into their needs and concerns, and can address these to improve understanding, buy-in and engagement.

* Recognise and reward diversity achievements and profile them, to raise the bar on activities.

* Take advantage of opportunities for quick wins that will support business goals.

* Keep up the momentum – managing diversity is a continuous process.

* Don't lose heart, stay cool and be patient. Changing things takes time, effort and persistence. You may lose a few battles on the way to winning the war.

* When something does not work, don't sweep it under the carpet, but learn from it –it may be the biggest boost to energise progress.

* When you experience a successful outcome, celebrate it.

* Make sure managing diversity is not marginalised as an HR issue –it belongs to everyone.

REFERENCES

ANDERSON, T. and METCALF, H. (2004)

Diversity: stacking up the evidence. London: Chartered Institute of Personnel and Development.

DEPARTMENT OF TRADE AND INDUSTRY. (2005)

Equality and diversity: the way ahead. London: HMSO. Available at: http://www.dti.gov.uk/er/equality/ [Accessed: 13 December, 2005].

EASTERBY-SMITH, M., THORPE, R. and LOWE, A. (2002)

Management research: an introduction. 2nd ed. London: Sage.

EDEN, C. and HUXHAM, C. (1996)

'Action research for management research'. *British Journal of Management.* Vol 7, No 1. pp75–86.

GLASER, B and STRAUSS, A. (1967)

The discovery of grounded theory. New York: Aldine de Gruyter.

HONEY, P. and MUMFORD, A. (1992)

A manual of learning styles. 3rd ed. Maidenhead: Peter Honey.

HUSSERL, E. (1946)

'Phenomenology' in *Encyclopaedia Britannica.* 14th ed. Vol. 17, pp 699–702.

KANDOLA, R. and FULLERTON, J. (1994)

Managing the mosaic: diversity in action. London: Institute of Personnel and Development.

KOLB, D.A. (1984)

Experiential learning: experience as the source of learning and development. Englewood-Cliffs, NJ: Prentice Hall.

LEIGHTON, P (2004)

Discrimination and the law: does the system suit the purpose? London: Chartered Institute of Personnel and Development.

MAYO, E. (1945)

The social problems of an industrial civilisation. Boston, MA: Harvard University.

MCNIFF, J. and WHITEHEAD, J. (2002)

Action research: principles and practice. 2nd ed. London: Routledge.

MOLLOY, E. and WHITTINGTON, R (2005)

HR: making change happen. London: Chartered Insitute of Personnel and Development.

MULHOLLAND, G., ÖZBILGIN, M. and WORMAN, D. (2005)

Managing diversity: linking theory and practice to business performance. Change Agenda. London: Chartered Institute of Personnel and Development. Available at: http://www.cipd.co.uk/subjects/dvsequl/general/mandivlink0405.htm [Accessed 13 December 2005].

PURCELL, J., SWART, J., KINNIE, N., HUTCHINSON, S. and RAYTON, B. (2003)

Understanding the people and performance link: Unlocking the black box. London: Chartered Institute of Personnel and Development.

REASON, P. and BRADBURY, H. Eds. (2001)

Handbook of action research: participative inquiry and practice. London: Sage.

REASON, P. and ROWAN, J. (1981)

Human inquiry: a sourcebook of new paradigm research. Chichester: Wiley.

REES, D. (2004)

Women in the boardroom: a bird's eye view. Change Agenda. London: Chartered Institute of Personnel and Development. Available at: http://www.cipd.co.uk/NR/rdonlyres/5CA22125-06A8-48AA-8D5D-7A5AAE6F529C/0/3052cawmnbrdrm.pdf [Accessed 7 April 2006].

TATLI, A. ÖZBILGIN M., MULHOLLAND, G. and WORMAN, D (2006)

Managing diversity: measuring success. Change Agenda. London: Chartered Institute of Personnel and Development. Available at: http://www.cipd.co.uk/NR/rdonlyres/809E744B–5018-4592-9544-ADC2A311937F/0/mandiversca0306.pdf [Accessed 30 March 2006].

THOMAS TAYLOR, W. PIASECKA, A. and WORMAN, D. (2005)

Managing diversity: learning by doing. Change Agenda. London: Chartered Institute of Personnel and Development.Available at: http://www.cipd.co.uk/subjects/dvsequl/general/mandivlrnbydo0605.htm?IsSrchRes=1 [Accessed 13 December 2005].

TORBERT, W.R. (1991)

The power of balance: transforming self, society, and scientific inquiry. Newbury Park, CA: Sage.

WORMAN, D. BLAND, A. and CHASE, P. (2005)

Managing diversity: people make the difference at work – but everyone is different. Guide. London: Chartered Institute of Personnel and Development. Available at: http://www.cipd.co.uk/NR/rdonlyres/493588D2-1BB3-43A8-9D34-3916C5FC868C/0/mandivers0305.pdf [Accessed 30 March 2006].

YIN, R.K. (1989)

Case study research: design and methods. Newbury Park, CA: London: Sage.

Learning Resources Centre